The Really Wicked Droning Wasp and
other things that bite and sting

A DORLING KINDERSLEY BOOK

Project Editor Caroline Bingham
Art Editor Mike Buckley
Extra design help Anna Benckert,
Ivan Finnegan, Karen Lieberman

Deputy Managing Editor Mary Ling
Senior Art Editor Jane Horne

Production David Hyde
Picture research Ingrid Nilsson

**Photography, at risk to life
and limb, by** Frank Greenaway
and Kim Taylor

First published in Great Britain in 1996
by Dorling Kindersley Limited,
9 Henrietta Street, London WC2E 8PS

Copyright © 1996 Dorling Kindersley Limited

A CIP catalogue record for this book
is available from the British Library.

ISBN: 0-7513-5461-9

Colour reproduction by Colourscan
Printed and bound in Italy by L.E.G.O.

The publisher would like to thank the following
for their kind permission to reproduce their
photographs:

t top, b bottom, l left, r right, c centre.

Bruce Coleman/Dr Frieder Sauer 11br/
Jan Taylor 12bl/Kim Taylor 8tr, 9br, 10tr, 10/11bc;
NHPA/Anthony Bannister 4bl, 20tr/
Stephen Dalton 20b/Rod Planck 21tr; Oxford
Scientific Films/London Scientific Films 13br/Harold
Taylor 12tr, cr, br; Premaphotos/
R.A. Preston-Mafham 10bl 20c.

Hairy Horrors
Page 14

The Tail End
Page 18

Cut and Stab
Page 20

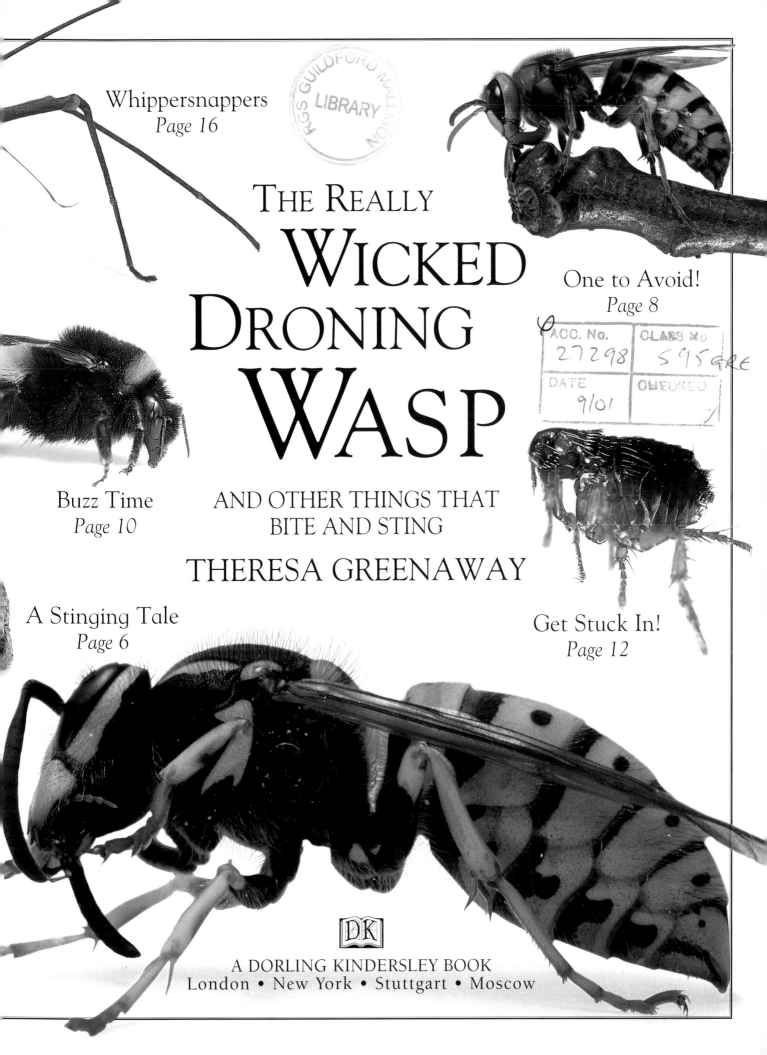

Whippersnappers
Page 16

THE REALLY
WICKED
DRONING
WASP

One to Avoid!
Page 8

Buzz Time
Page 10

AND OTHER THINGS THAT
BITE AND STING

THERESA GREENAWAY

A Stinging Tale
Page 6

Get Stuck In!
Page 12

DK

A DORLING KINDERSLEY BOOK
London • New York • Stuttgart • Moscow

A STINGING TALE

Wasps are really annoying, stinging insects, especially in hot weather at the end of summer. But wasps are not all bad. Every day, wasps catch insects, including many that are pests, to feed to their young – the wasp larvae.

Many wasps are social insects, living in nests with some 2,000 others. The nests are made from chewed-up wood.

Tropical wasp

A wasp nest contains female workers, drones (or male wasps), and a queen. Workers have stings to use in self-defence and to paralyse or kill their prey.

A jewel wasp's body-casing gleams like metal in sunlight.

Jewel wasp

German wasp, queen

Ichneuman wasps lay eggs inside other insects. The larvae feed on their host before chewing a way out.

Ichneuman wasp

Wasps

The jewel wasp seizes a cricket with fearsome jaws and stings deep into its nerve centre to paralyse it.

Jewel wasp

Sometimes a jewel wasp's catch is dragged into a burrow, where the wasp lays an egg in it. It's good food for the young!

Unlike bees, wasps have straight stings and can sting again and again.

Only the queen lays eggs. After setting up a nest, she feeds her first batch of larvae. As adults, they take over the task of rearing young wasps.

7

ONE TO AVOID!

Their size and the noise of their wings strikes terror into the heart of anyone who has a close encounter with a humming hornet, a large wasp. But don't worry; hornets usually live and hunt in woodlands, not in houses.

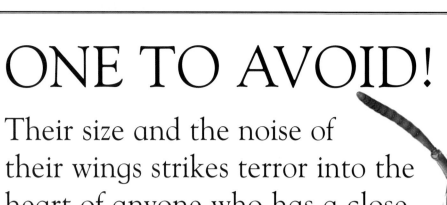

Hornet in flight

A hornet is the biggest stinging insect in the world.

Hornet

Watch out for the sting in the tail.

Hornets search for insect prey using large compound eyes and sensitive antennae. Prey is taken to the nest and chewed up, then fed to the hornet young, or grubs.

A hornet isn't afraid of wasps and bees. It can cut them in half with one swipe of its powerful, scissor-like jaws.

Hornet resting on acorn

Because it's so large, a hornet's sting hurts a lot. Fortunately, hornets only sting humans if they feel threatened.

Not all hornets have the ability to sting. This drone, or male, looks fierce, but he doesn't have a sting.

Hornet workers can grow up to 33 mm in length!

Male hornet

BUZZ TIME

Bees are useful. They pollinate flowers and many provide honey. But be careful! Bees can sting, and that's a powerful weapon.

Honey-bee worker

Female bee

As a bee stings, a cocktail of chemicals is pumped from a venom sac into the wound.

Honey-bees live in enormous colonies that may contain some 50,000 bees.

Not all bees live in colonies. Some are solitary, with each female bee making her own small nest.

A bumble-bee's wings beat about 200 times each second!

It looks too heavy to fly, but it reaches 16 kph!

The hairy carder-bee, a small type of bumble-bee, collects nectar from flowers to feed to its larvae.

Carder-bee

Honey-bee in flight

Honey-bees have barbed stings. Once a bee uses its sting, it cannot pull it out. As the bee flies away, part of its insides are pulled out. The bee will die.

Honey-bee stinging

As honey-bees fly along, their two pairs of wings make a distinctive buzz.

Using its sting means certain death for the bee.

GET STUCK IN!

All sorts of awful parasites live on the outside of many animals, even on us. They are looking for blood to suck, and they have ways of making sure they stay with their host.

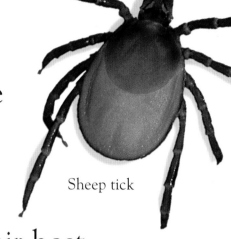
Sheep tick

Flea

Sheep ticks will only have three meals in their lifetime. For each one, they climb up a grass stem and grab on to a passing animal.

Sheep tick

A flea's body is flattened from side to side, so it can race through its host's fur.

Ticks are related to spiders. Adults have eight legs.

Kangaroo tick

A tick anchors itself to the host's skin with a toothed stabber called a hypostome.

It takes a few days for a tick to completely fill up with blood. It becomes so swollen, it starts to look like a bean.

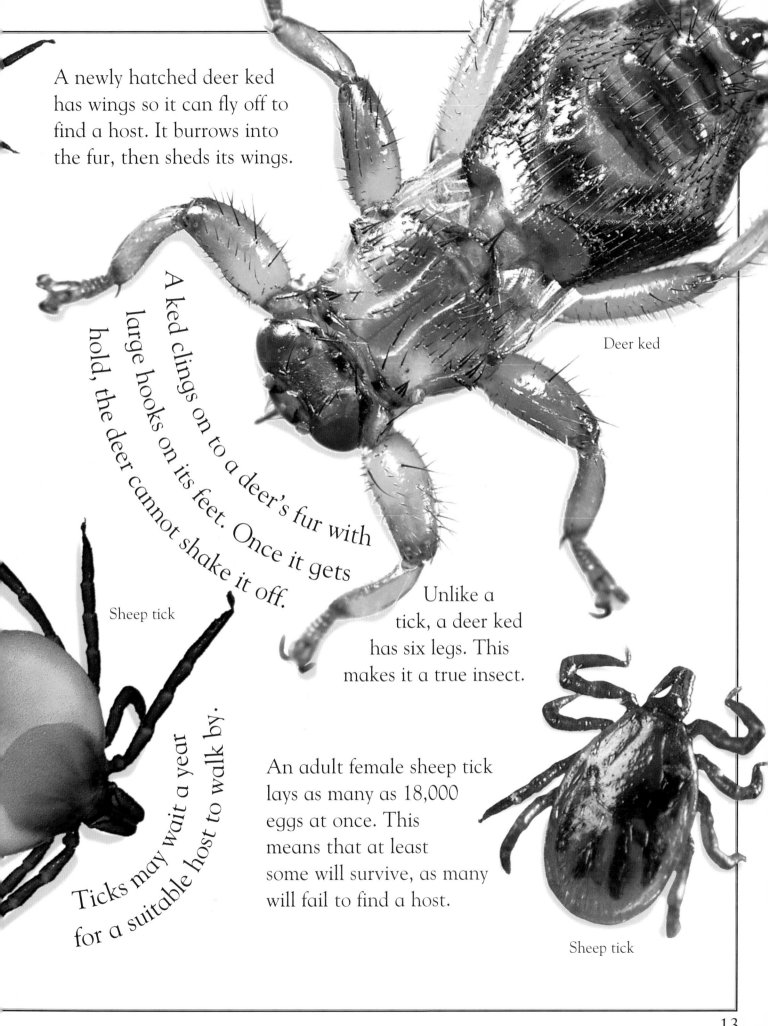

A newly hatched deer ked has wings so it can fly off to find a host. It burrows into the fur, then sheds its wings.

Deer ked

A ked clings on to a deer's fur with large hooks on its feet. Once it gets hold, the deer cannot shake it off.

Sheep tick

Unlike a tick, a deer ked has six legs. This makes it a true insect.

Ticks may wait a year for a suitable host to walk by.

An adult female sheep tick lays as many as 18,000 eggs at once. This means that at least some will survive, as many will fail to find a host.

Sheep tick

HAIRY HORRORS

How can a juicy caterpillar avoid ending up as some other animal's dinner? Surprisingly, hairs can help – from hairs that snap off to hairs that inject poisonous fluids.

A tropical lappet moth caterpillar

Caterpillar after moult

This caterpillar is so hairy that a bird trying to peck it up just gets a beakful of hairs.

A tropical tiger moth caterpillar

A tropical tiger moth caterpillar is truly nasty. Just brushing its hairs causes skin sores and an incurable arthritis in nearby joints.

When the bright yellow caterpillar moults, its next hairy jacket is sombre grey.

Colonial
caterpillars
keep together
and produce
toxins if
touched.

Colonial
caterpillars

When a predator approaches, colonial caterpillars
fling back their heads and thrash about wildly.
The predator is tricked into thinking
it's facing one large animal.

A tropical
emperor moth
caterpillar

This alarming
caterpillar has long, sticky hairs,
making it unpleasant for a predator
to eat. The predator will only try once!

WHIPPERSNAPPERS

False whip scorpions are weird creatures that hunt at night and hide in the day. Because of this they are rarely seen, even in the tropics where most of them live.

Even the largest of these beasts can fold up its long legs and vanish into a surprisingly narrow crack.

Sharp spines on the front palps hold prey steady. The mangled corpse

Spiny front grabbers called palps seize and crush up live prey. Then bits of food are passed to the jaws.

With their eight spindly legs, they are alarming to look at, but they are not poisonous.

Long front legs reach out to feel the way.

Six of the eight legs are used for running – very fast. The two incredibly long and thin legs at the front are used just like antennae.

From tip to tip the legs reach 16 cm.

The leggy creatures climb easily over logs or rocks to hunt for insect prey.

scorpion's strong jaws.

up in the false whip

Prowling by night, these fierce predators will rush at and attack anything with their fearsome palps. They'd give you a sharp nip if they got close enough.

is then chewed

THE TAIL END

A large, apparently deadly scorpion frequently stars in scary films, but in fact, it's the small kinds that are the most dangerous – and only about 50 of the 1,200 species of scorpions are even likely to be dangerous to people.

Imperial scorpion

A scorpion's two eyes may look beady, but its sight is poor. It can only tell the difference between light and dark.

Pincers are used to hold down and rip apart a juicy grasshopper or a tasty centipede.

Scorpions have eight legs to run with and a huge pair of pincers. They use these pincers like hands, gripping prey.

The venom of one African scorpion can kill a person within seven hours. Venom is carried in a sting at the tip of the tail.

Desert scorpion

A scorpion can survive without water for three months, and without food for twelve months!

Scorpion with babies

A scorpion gives birth to lots of tiny scorpions. They climb on their mother's back for two weeks, until they are stronger.

CUT AND STAB

Only female horseflies are bloodthirsty pirates. They need the nutrients in blood to be able to make their eggs. Male horseflies prefer to spend their days buzzing lazily about, sipping nectar from flowers.

Horsefly cleaning its proboscis

To get blood, a female horsefly stabs into her victim's skin with a sharp, stout tube called a proboscis.

Horsefly

A horsefly leaves its victim with a large and painful swelling.

Horsefly

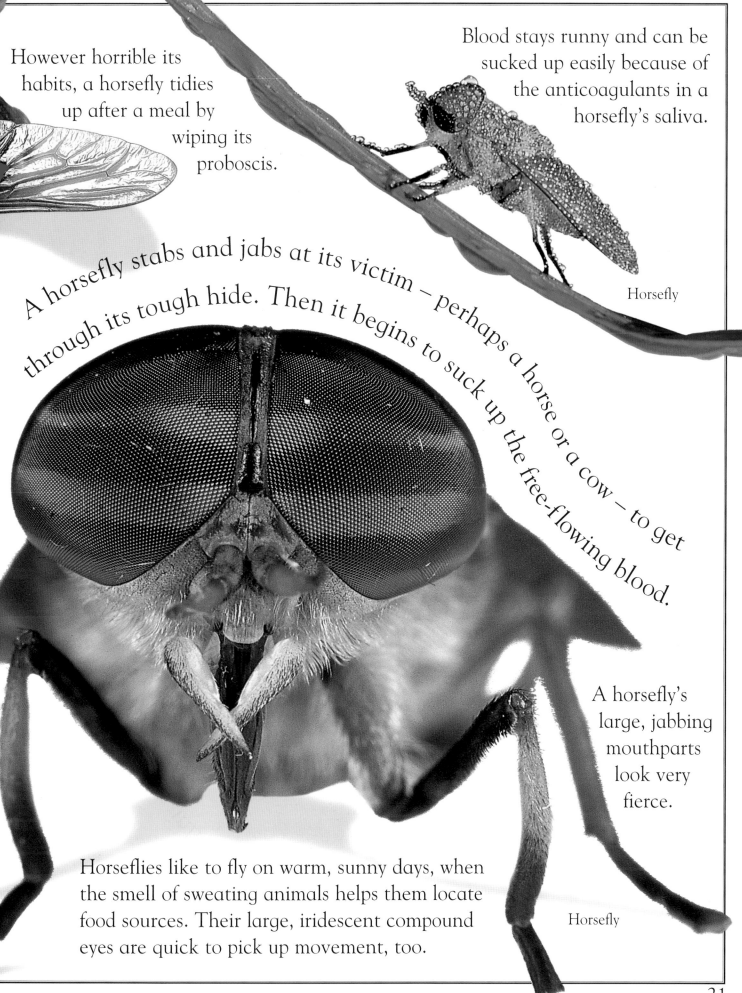

However horrible its habits, a horsefly tidies up after a meal by wiping its proboscis.

Blood stays runny and can be sucked up easily because of the anticoagulants in a horsefly's saliva.

Horsefly

A horsefly stabs and jabs at its victim – perhaps a horse or a cow – to get through its tough hide. Then it begins to suck up the free-flowing blood.

A horsefly's large, jabbing mouthparts look very fierce.

Horseflies like to fly on warm, sunny days, when the smell of sweating animals helps them locate food sources. Their large, iridescent compound eyes are quick to pick up movement, too.

Horsefly

21